Cross-country Skiing

Hans Brunner   Alois Kälin

Cross-country Skiing

Translated and adapted by Wolfgang E. Ruck from
Ski-Langlauf für Meister und Geniesser

McGraw-Hill Ryerson Limited

Toronto   Montreal   New York   London   Sydney   Johannesburg   Mexico   Panama

Düsseldorf   Singapore   Rio de Janeiro   Kuala Lumpur   New Delhi

Cross-country Skiing

Translated from Ski-Langlauf für Meister und Geniesser
by arrangement with Benziger Verlag

© 1969 Benziger Verlag, Zürich, Köln

Drawings by Hans Brunner
Photographs:
Berger Ernst, Zurich   18
Bruell Pressbild, Zurich   10, 19, 29, 31, 64, 79,
also Cover
Brunner Hans, Magglingen   58
Kälin Carl, Dr., Einsiedeln/Egg   6
Kälin Franz, Einsiedeln   77
Photo ETS, Magglingen   34
Photo Press, Zurich   78
Ruck, Wolfgang E., Mississauga, Ontario   11, 13, 14, 15, 16, 17, 53, 56, 57, 58, 59

Ren-Film, Einsiedeln, all action sequence photography
as well as the photographs on pages   16, 21, 22, 24, 40, 55, 68, 69, 71, 80

Library of Congress Catalog Card Number 72-9533

ISBN 0-07-077478-1

 2345678910   D-72   109876543

Printed and bound in Canada

Foreword by Marc Hodler
President of the International Ski Federation (FIS)

Inadequate physical activity is an all-too-common ailment of our modern age. When over-emphasis on machines, automation and technology prevents man from obtaining sufficiently stimulating activity for muscle, heart and lungs, he must find a balancing substitute to maintain his physical health. Cross-country skiing is ideally suited to fulfill his need for exercise. Practised in Scandinavian countries for decades, this sport is on the verge of becoming the most popular form of winter recreation in the world. This is not surprising, for cross-country skiing combines the healthful benefits of physical activity and effort with the overwhelming peace and beauty of the winter landscape.

With the publication of this book, Hans Brunner and Alois Kälin will not only win new friends for the sport but also provide an excellent source of information for the veteran skier. Both authors are experts in the field with many years of top-level experience. As a former competitor and subsequent official, Hans Brunner has gained the friendship and respect of crosscountry experts all over the world. The experience of Alois Kälin, a talented skier who has impressed even the Scandinavian elite over the years, complements the expertise of Hans Brunner with the latest advances in technique and knowledge of training and competition. For their work and efforts in helping to spread this excellent sport in a knowledgeable manner, I wish to express my sincerest appreciation. I am aware, of course, that they do not expect words of gratitude. The imminent success and growth in popularity of their favourite sport will most certainly be their best reward.

Marc Hodler

Contents

Translator's note

It is hoped that the English version of this informative manual will help more people to enjoy the simple, i n e x p e n s i v e and invigorating winter sport of cross-country skiing. This sport is particularly well suited to our long winters and vast open spaces and it satisfies all the principles of individualized recreation. There are no age or sex barriers—anyone who can walk can ski cross-country. It is safe and inexpensive; snow and a stretch of open country are the only facilities required. It can be for groups, families or loners; the individual sets his own pace. Cross-country skiing can be a pleasant form of recreation, part of an all-round fitness training programme, or a challenging athletic competition, in which form it is one of the most demanding of all sports. Above all, skiing cross-country brings man back into direct physical contact with the world of nature, creating an often neglected but much-needed harmony between man and his environment.

The chapters on equipment and waxing have been expanded somewhat over the original Swiss edition in anticipation of the need for more detailed information in these areas. Approximate English equivalents are given for distances in metric units. Also the Fahrenheit equivalents of Centigrade degrees of temperature have been added.

Introduction

It is not our aim to write a long, involved textbook, but simply to pass on our knowledge and experience. Beginners and advanced skiers alike should find the suggestions in this book easy to follow and to put into practice.

We have attempted to explain things simply and have avoided technical terminology where possible. We do not wish to over-analyze, for example, by dividing the Stride into Push, Swing and Glide phases. Where simple instructions are more easily understood, we even refrain from emphasizing the distinction between body and equipment. Our own teaching experience has shown us the advantages of this approach.

The emphasis of this book is on technique. Since it is impossible to attain optimal style without an appropriate measure of physical fitness and condition, some advice is given on preparatory training.

Considerable space is allotted to waxing and waxes. Where helpful to the cross-country skier, extra information and practical tips have been included.

Chapter 1   Equipment

Cross-country equipment is considerably lighter and less expensive than downhill equipment. The equipment you choose will depend on your aims. Does your interest lie in touring, competition, fitness training, or all-round recreation? This decision should be made *before* purchasing skis and equipment.

1. Skis

Cross-country skis come in various lengths (measured in centimeters), widths (measured in millimeters), and degrees of flexibility (i.e. stiffness). Attempts are being made to create an all-synthetic ski which does not require waxing. However, none has so far been able to duplicate the feel and effectiveness of properly-waxed laminated wood skis.

■ Length
Skis come in 5cm. intervals from 180 to 220 cm. Shorter skis are available for children. The ski tip should reach to mid-palm when standing erect, arm stretched over the head. When in doubt, choose a ski 5 cm. too short rather than 5 cm. too long. Shorter skis are easier to control; longer skis facilitate a long glide.

■ Width
Your purpose will determine which width to choose.

Racing skis (54-56 mm.) are best suited for the skilful competitor and well-prepared tracks.

All-round skis (57-60 mm.) are sometimes used for racing or training. The increased surface area improves balance. They are ideal for general recreation including fitness-training and light touring.

Touring skis (62-66 mm.) are heavier, generally being used for touring in open, untracked country and when carrying a heavy rucksack on extended outings.

■ Flexibility

When the ski is weighted, the tension in the camber should allow the ski to flatten along its entire length but still give a noticeable spring to the push-off. A heavy skier requires more tension than a light skier. Regularly examine the bases of your skis: blank areas under the bindings indicate insufficient tension, blank areas under ski tip and heel indicate excessive tension. Over long distances, a ski which is too flexible loses wax rapidly and the skier tires quickly due to lack of spring in the skis. On the other hand, a stiff ski "plows" into moguls, slowing the skier down, and slips on the push-off since the waxed base under the bindings fails to make good contact with the snow. The skis must respond lively under pressure but they should not be stiff.

■ Base and edges

A birch base holds dry wax best and is very fast on powder snow at low temperatures. The harder hickory base is more resistant to wear but does not hold wax as well. Synthetic bases are very wear-resistant but require even more wax than hickory. Hard, wear resistant edges are an asset when edging on a traverse or making turns. For competition and under optimal conditions, a birch base is advantageous. For fitness training and all-round use, a hickory base would seem desirable. Synthetic bases, on the other hand, require minimal care.

■ Hints for buying skis

— Check both skis for equal camber. Place skis side by side on the floor and observe from the side: a difference of more than ¼ in. in the height of the camber at the bindings will seriously hamper good style.

— Test the tension (flexibility) of the camber. Press skis together at the middle, base to base, with one hand. As the bases come together, tension should increase; the last ½ inch between them should offer the greatest resistance.

— Bases pressed together should be in contact along the entire length of the skis. The ski tips should not rise as a result.

— Ski tips should be quite flexible to allow the ski to track well by conforming and adapting easily to slight variations in the track structure. The tail end of the skis should be less flexible but not too stiff.

— Examine for warping by sighting with one eye from ski tip to heel along the groove in the ski base.

■ Care

— Insufficient tension in an otherwise well-built ski or tension diminished by much use can often be corrected by gently warming the ski base under the binding with the waxing torch.

— Hickory and birch bases must be thoroughly impregnated with base tar before using. Burn Grundvalla *carefully* into birch as birch reacts strongly to heat.

Before applying base tar, plane the base smooth with a scraper blade.

— Sand and re-varnish chips and scratches in the upper surface of the ski. Snow sticks to exposed areas and moisture seeps into raw wood causing the skis to warp.

— Before storing skis for the summer, clean bases thoroughly and apply a fresh coating of Grundvalla. Store the skis in a cool, not too dry, location.

■ Spare ski-tip

If a ski breaks, it usually breaks at the tip. A spare ski tip taken along on extended cross-country trips can save many weary hours of trudging through deep snow on foot. The size of the spare tip

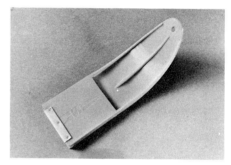

should match the width of the skis. Adjustable versions which can be quickly and easily fitted on different sized skis are also available.

2. Bindings

Cross-country bindings are extremely light and are designed to allow the heels to lift freely off the ski. Boots and bindings are standardized. Therefore bring your boots when buying bindings. The classical "rat-trap" binding and its one-piece variation are the most effective for competition and light touring. Cable bindings are used with the heavier touring skis and boots. They give more control over the skis on downhill stretches but less freedom of movement at the heel. The spikes on the rat-trap binding must fit into corresponding holes drilled into the projecting sole of the boot.

The heel plate is either made of rubber alone or a rubber cup set into a metal base plate. The inverted and compressible rubber cup springs back into shape when the heel is lifted and thus prevents snow from clumping under the boot. The metal base plate often has sharp projections which dig into the boot heel and prevent the heel from slipping sideways off the ski.

Classical "rat-trap" binding

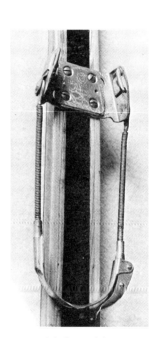

Light cable binding

One-piece "rat-trap" binding

3. Boots

Competition and light touring boots resemble track shoes. They are low-cut, of light construction, and have a very flexible sole. The spring clamp of the rat trap binding fits tightly over the projecting sole at the toe. Touring boots are higher, heavier, and often warmer. They usually have a groove at the heel for the cable binding.

Competition boot

Light touring boot

Touring boot

Cross-country boots must fit snugly but comfortably. Boots which are too large reduce control over the skis. Short or tight boots cause painful blisters and reduce warmth-giving blood circulation in feet and toes. When trying boots for size, wear the same stockings and socks that you intend to use on the trail. Avoid boots which form stiff ridges over the toes when the heel is lifted. Soles and uppers should be very flexible to allow for maximum heel lift and at the same time provide good support. Both leather and all-rubber construction is available. The latter require minimal care. They may be somewhat warmer and drier in extremely cold or wet weather, but moisture tends to accumulate inside the boot, often nullifying these advantages. The former is usually more rugged and "breathes" well, but requires good care and occasional water-proofing treatment with appro-

15

priate compounds. A thin, light and inexpensive rubber "overshoe" may be worn over leather boots in very wet and cold situations. A thick wool sock pulled over the boot is even more effective against extreme cold.

Never place boots near a hot stove, open fire, or in direct sunlight to dry. The leather tends to crack and stiffen if exposed to heat. A warm, well-ventilated room is more suitable.

4. Poles

Cross country ski poles should be light and flexible. Light metal (alloy), bamboo, tonkin and fiberglass construction is available. As with skis, the poles should respond lively under pressure.

Length. Maximum length is 12 inches less than the skier's height. Poles which are too long hinder good style and prevent fast, well-placed pole work often necessary in varied terrain.

Loops. Poles should have adjustable loops. Adjust them so that the hand can be opened without losing the pole behind.

Tips: These should be sharp and are usually angled to provide maximum grip on the snow throughout the pole action.

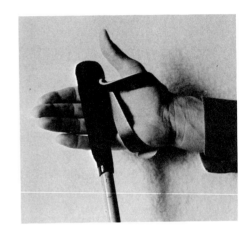

Baskets. Baskets should be light, solidly attached, and not too small. Taping the joints of bamboo and tonkin poles helps prevent their breaking.

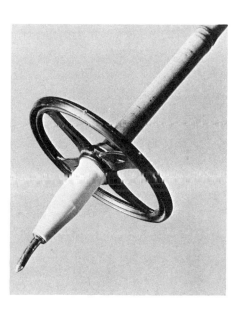

5. Clothing

Warm, sweat-absorbing underwear is absolutely necessary. Scandinavians prefer net underwear which creates an insulating layer of air between skin and clothing. A warm shirt, turtle-neck, or pullover is worn under a wind-proof shell in cold weather. Remember that clothing must "breathe" to prevent accumulation of moisture which can result in rapid cooling and even freezing. Light knickers provide maximum freedom for knee action and are ideal for the cross-country style. With knickers are worn long, warm, woollen stockings which should fit snugly but not too tightly at the knees. For sensitive feet, a nylon or silk sock worn inside the stockings will help prevent blisters and keep the feet warm.

Special close-fitting gloves of

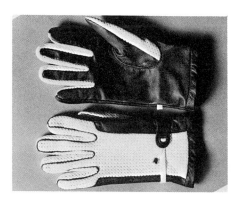

tough, pliable reindeer hide are most used by cross country skiers. A somewhat larger glove worn over these keeps the fingers warm in extreme cold.

A warm wool touque and/or head band prevent excessive heat loss and keep the ears warm.

Warm and properly-fitting clothing is mandatory. Shirts which ride up on the back and stockings which slide down the leg expose sensitive areas to cold and may result in cramps and even illness.

"Warmth gives strength" is a basic principle governing all sports and it applies to cross-country skiing in particular.

Chapter 2 Cross-country technique

The following principles of cross-country technique apply to everyone—to the recreational skier and touring enthusiast as well as to the most ambitious competitor.
Although good cross-country technique is the most natural and easiest, it cannot be learned by studying theory alone. One must get the "feel" of it; and this by skiing, skiing and more skiing. *How* to ski is described on the following pages.

Suggestions printed in blue are directed mainly at the advanced skier and competitor. Of course, they may be useful to the novice also. It is advised, however, that beginners concentrate on learning the fundamentals first. Once the basic movements come automatically and without conscious effort, these extra hints will assume greater significance. The key to

good technique lies in the basic fundamentals, and the success of all great Nordic skiers is a direct result of their ability to master and apply these principles most effectively.

The strides

1. The Diagonal Stride

Called "diagonal" because the limbs work in a diagonal fashion similar to walking (i.e. right arm forward, left leg forward), the Diagonal Stride forms the basis of all cross-country technique.
Concentrate on the following three principles:

■ Always glide on one ski
A good skier glides relaxed and in perfect balance on *one* ski. Throughout the glide, the entire body weight is centered over the gliding ski.

The balanced glide on *one* ski

— allows momentarily inactive parts of the body to relax,
— prevents the ski from side-slipping off the track,
— leaves the skier free to initiate other movements in the horizontal plane (such as changes in direction, etc.)

Front view

■ **Center the weight over (not behind) the ski**

Proper weighting *over* the ski is characterized by a marked forward lean. The lean is facilitated by strongly flexing the knee of the glide leg. (The boot tip, but not the stockings, should just be visible below the knee.)

Proper weighting *over* the ski
- allows development of maximum pulling force by the arms
- prepares the skier for movement changes in the vertical plane, such as changes in stride length and rate (cadence) on uphill stretches, and properly timed and executed action on moguls (crests and troughs).

Over the ski

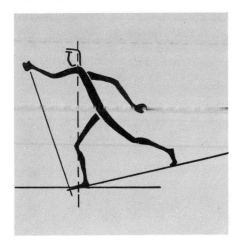

Behind the ski (wrong)

Bent knee (detail)

■ Stretch completely and forcefully with each stride

A complete and forceful stretch (extension) is made possible by:

1 A quick forward and upward swing of the arm from the shoulder which

2 facilitates powerful hip extension and the almost simultaneous extension of

3 the knee

4 the ankle

5 and the foot (with a final strong push-off from the toes).

This means that the striding action is initiated by the body, *not* the limbs. An effective stride consequently does not depend on leg length but rather on the quality of *hip extension.*

Extension (stretch)

Wind-up

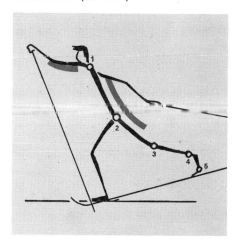

Some competitors maintain a fairly upright stance, others ski in a more bent-over fashion. The body position will depend on the physical attributes of the skier and determines his personal style. Both variations are equally effective provided the hips come well forward with the stretch action.

Also keep in mind the following important points:

■ The push-off
The stretch action is completed with a powerful final push from the toes. This finishing push is of utmost importance. The extended leg swings back loosely and relaxed and then comes forward again for the next stride.

■ The leg swing
Theorists often debate whether the ski should be kept off the snow as the leg is swung forward, or whether it should be kept in contact with the track. In practice, the former is more efficient and eiegant on a good, hard track and with properly waxed skis. On poorly tracked, icy, or otherwise difficult snow and on skis which are too fast, it is advantageous to slide the ski (unweighted of course) forward on the snow.

Extension with toe push-off

Relaxed leg swing

■ Pole action
The pole is planted at a level even with the opposite foot. The tip points backwards. The pole action *follows* the stretch, that is, a split second after the push-off from the ski is initiated. The arms work in a

vertical plane parallel to the direction of travel. The hand on the pole

grip is brought low past the knee of the glide leg.

The pole is planted about 6 inches wide of the near ski. The grip remains in the vertical plane of the pole action during the pull and thrust. However, it is advantageous to bring the grip slightly in towards the skis with the final backward thrust of the hand.

Do not grasp the pole too tightly. Relax the fingers during the end-thrust and let the sling carry the pole.

The hands also pass low during the forward recovery swing. Relax the arms and let them hang loosely whenever they are not actively working. Hands kept high and at hip level indicate poor balance and tire the arms quickly.

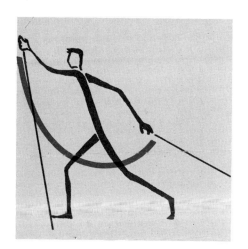

Path of hand and grip

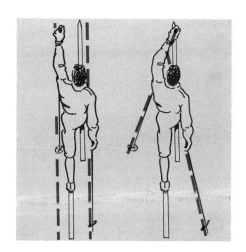

Arms work parallel to direction of travel

Common mistake: Hands pulled towards the skis in front cause poles to be planted too far out

2. The Pendulum Stride

Also known as the Finn Stride, the Pendulum Stride is a variation of the Diagonal Stride.

The principles of gliding on *one* ski, centering the weight *over* the ski, and forceful *stretch* action also apply to the Pendulum Stride. The poling action however, is different from that of the Diagonal Stride: instead of one pole plant with each stride, *two* pole plants are made

every *four* strides. On strides 1 and 2, the poles are swung forward in pendulum fashion and a plant is made on each side for the slightly longer third and fourth strides.

The Pendulum Stride is extremely useful in learning. It forces the arms and legs to work indepen-

dently and brings powerful hip action into play. Only when properly executed is the Pendulum Stride as effective as the Diagonal Stride.

By turning the shoulders slightly on the somewhat longer third and fourth strides, the pole thrust may be effectively extended. The Pendulum Stride is mostly used on gentle uphill stretches to give tired arms a rest.

■ The Swedish Three-Stroke

This variation of the Pendulum Stride has made its appearance only recently. In the Three-Stroke, *three* pole plants are made every *four* strides, or, stated another way, *one* pole plant is *omitted* every four strides. It is always the same pole which is left out, either the right or the left.

The Three-Stroke is used in the same kind of situations as the Finn Stride.

The Three-Stroke is particularly useful when traversing (crossing) a slope. Here the pole plant on the *uphill* side is omitted.

3. The Combined Strides
(strides combined with the Double-Pole Push)

The striding action is the same as in the Diagonal Stride.

■ The Double-Pole Push

Position at pole plant: the arms are slightly bent at the elbow, hands held shoulder-width apart, and pole tips are pointed back towards the feet.

The push: arms are momentarily stiffened, the upper body folds at the waist and comes down and forward over the poles. The hands push back low. The end-thrust should be especially quick and powerful.

With the final thrust, the hands are pressed together behind the body. Simultaneously, the hips are thrust forward resulting in a slight backward lean. (A backward lean tends to increase speed.)
When the arms are very tired, simply collapsing the upper body over the slightly bent and stiffened arms will result in an effective Double-Pole Push.

■ The One-Stride

(combination of one stride with a double-pole push). Important: the stride comes *first*. The poling action *follows* the push-off from the ski. In other words: a normal stride initiates the glide, and the momentum of the glide is reinforced by the subsequent double-pole push.

In the One-Stride, the same push-off leg may be used repeatedly, or left and right legs may be alternated.

Very important for the effectiveness of the double-pole push is the body position at the instant of pole plant. The skier must be in position to "fold over" quickly and initiate the pole thrust immediately.

Proper body position is attained by:
- assuming a marked forward lean, by
- strongly flexing the knee of the glide leg,
- bringing the hips well forward,
- bending the elbows slightly.

Under difficult snow or track conditions, it is advantageous to shorten the time span between the stride and the initiation of the double-pole push. The poling action then follows the stride almost simultaneously.

Whether the push-off is made repeatedly from the same leg, or whether it is alternated, will depend on the terrain. When traversing a slope, for instance, the *uphill* ski is used for the push-off, and the *downhill* ski becomes the glide ski.

■ The Two-Stride
(combination of two strides with a double-pole push)

The movement sequence of the Two-Stride is similar to that of the One-Stride. However, an extra stride is taken between the double-poling action. This in-between stride should not be a hasty step, but rather a strong, gliding stride with powerful hip action. It allows more time to swing the ski poles forward into a good position for the plant. The Two-Stride is particularly effective on a hard, fast, and gently declining track.

In this version of the Two-Stride, the same leg is used repeatedly for the push-off leading into the double-pole push.

■ **The Three-Stride**
(combination of three strides with
a double-pole push)
This stride is not highly effective
and is not described here.

33

Chapter 3 Skiing in varied terrain

The more skilfully a skier adapts his technique to the terrain, the more effective and effortless will be his progress. The successful cross-country skier is always an expert at adapting to changes in terrain. Adapting involves:

1. Choosing the stride

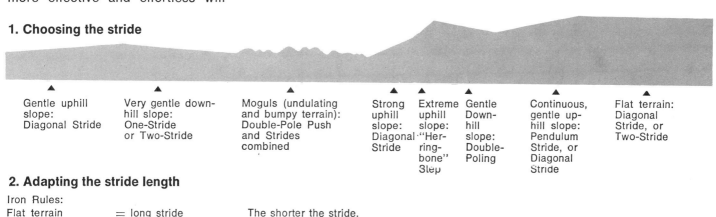

Gentle uphill slope:
Diagonal Stride

Very gentle down-hill slope:
One-Stride
or Two-Stride

Moguls (undulating and bumpy terrain):
Double-Pole Push and Strides combined

Strong uphill slope:
Diagonal Stride

Extreme uphill slope: "Her-ring-bone" Step

Gentle Down-hill slope:
Double-Poling

Continuous, gentle up-hill slope:
Pendulum Stride, or Diagonal Stride

Flat terrain:
Diagonal Stride, or Two-Stride

2. Adapting the stride length

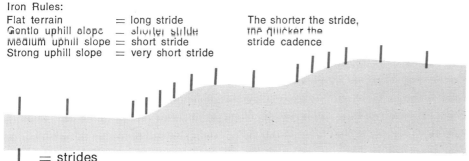

Iron Rules:

Flat terrain = long stride
Gentle uphill slope = shorter stride
Medium uphill slope = short stride
Strong uphill slope = very short stride

The shorter the stride, the quicker the stride cadence

| = strides

To be effective, the change from one stride to another must be made smoothly. It is important to shorten the stride early (not after the first slip) and not to lengthen the stride too soon.

3. Uphill technique

On a gentle uphill slope, the Diagonal and Pendulum Strides are most efficient. It is a mistake to revert to a "tourist stride" and simply "march" up an incline. Except for shortening the length and increasing the rate (cadence) of the stride appropriately, the technique for a gentle incline is the same as for flat terrain.

■ Striding uphill

The glide phase is short. To compensate, the pole work is faster. There is little time to swing the arms all the way forward and up since the poles must be planted again quickly. The hands on the grip follow through low.

The glide is omitted completely on steep inclines. The stride is shorter still and the arm action extended so that one of the poles is always in contact with the snow. This prevents the skis from slipping backwards.

It is very important to advance the hips, keeping the upper body erect and knees flexed. Weight is on the balls of the feet.

When competing in a race, one should start into an uphill stretch slowly and under control, then gradually increase the tempo and come out at the top of the slope quickly.

■ Jump-Step

When the slope becomes too steep for even the shortened Diagonal Stride, short "Jump-Steps" are used and the skier more or less "runs" up the incline. In the Jump-Step, the skis are lifted off the snow. This allows the snow to clump and stick to the base of the ski (due to the adhesive quality of the wax) without being rubbed off. The clumped snow dramatically improves the traction of the ski and enables the skier to climb relatively steep stretches.

When using the shortened Diagonal Stride and Jump-Steps on steep stretches, the knee of the attacking leg is flexed strongly and pushed forward.

The heels are no longer set down on the ski. The weight is on the balls of the feet, and the toes push off forcefully from the ski.

Occasionally, extremely steep terrain or skis which are too fast (slippery) will force the skier to use

■ The Herringbone step

Switch to the Herringbone *before* a big slip backward has spoiled a good start. The skis are spread apart in front just wide enough to prevent slipping. Strong pole work reinforces the leg action. It is of utmost importance to transfer the body weight quickly and completely from one ski to the other.

4. Downhill technique

Downhill stretches allow the skier to recover and catch his breath—provided that he is accustomed to skiing downhill on light cross-country skis. The loose binding between boot and ski does not provide much edge control over the skis for fast downhill manoeuvering. Considerable practice is required to master downhill turns on narrow skis. When possible, downhill stretches are skied "schuss" (straight down), and any changes in direction are made using the Step-Turn. Stem or Parallel-Turns are seldom used. To maximize control over the skis, the heels are weighted and a slight backward lean is assumed. The lean increases speed and is always used to advantage on gently declining stretches. The elbows are supported on the knees, the poles are clamped under the upper arms and the skis are left to track with minimum control.

When skiing small moguls, the skis are pressed strongly into the trough while maintaining the backward lean. The skis will then "shoot" out on the other side. Of course, one must be sure to stay with the skis in the process! Several moguls in succession are best crossed by "feathering" the crests with appropriate knee flexion, but every opportunity should be used to press the skis *through* the troughs in order to increase speed.

To decrease speed, stand up straight and spread the arms wide to increase wind resistance. When needed, the Snow Plow is quicker and more effective. In narrow passages, the poles may be used to slow down. Place both poles between the legs and weight them appropriately. However, do *not* sit on them with the entire body weight. By crossing the poles, chances of their breaking are decreased.

When traversing downhill, the *downhill* ski is weighted and the uphill shoulder, hip and ski are brought forward slightly. The hips are pushed in towards the slope and the upper body leans out, facing downhill. This gives the skis the necessary *edge* on the slope to permit controlled traversing.

By repeated "stepping-up" on the slope, it is possible to pick up speed on a traverse. Push off from the downhill ski and set the un-weighted uphill ski a shoulder-width higher on the slope. Then transfer the weight to the uphill ski and bring the push-off ski up and forward. Repeat.

5. Changing direction

■ Striding Turns

Wide, slow curves are skied using the Diagonal Stride. With each stride, the outside hip is brought forward and the outside ski is angled appropriately in the new direction.

■ Step-Turns

Abrupt and sharp turns are made most quickly and efficiently by "stepping" around the curve.

■ From the Stride

The now un-weighted push-off ski is quickly pulled even and brought forward directly for the next stride.

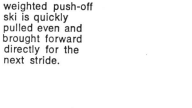

After an initiating Double-Pole Push, the outside ski is weighted, the inside shoulder leads into the new direction and the inside ski is angled in appropriately.

With a powerful Push-Off from the outside ski, the weight is transferred onto the inside ski.

The unweighted push-off ski must be brought forward for the next stride *very quickly*.

The downhill push-off ski must also be placed securely (no slipping!) to make the angling-in of the inside ski and the weight-transfer possible.

■ Step-Turns uphill

Time and energy may be saved by using the Step-Turn going uphill.

■ Step-turns at higher speeds

The initiating Double-Pole Push is omitted. At speeds which are not too fast, it is advantageous to plant the outside pole for increased support and stability.

■ Stem-Turns

In some situations, Stem-Turns are unavoidable. Execute Stem-Turns properly and in a relaxed manner. On cross-country skis, the Stem-Christie is the most effective Stem-Turn.

Chapter 4 Using terrain to advantage

A skilful skier uses variations in the terrain to increase speed and save energy. Here are some tricks which can be used again and again to help the skier cover irregular terrain more efficiently.

The eyes continually scan and assess the terrain ahead. The type of stride and the stride length are chosen accordingly.

■ Placing the skis

The ski must always be set down so that maximum contact is made between ski base and snow. The ski must be stable and provide a solid base for a powerful Push-Off.

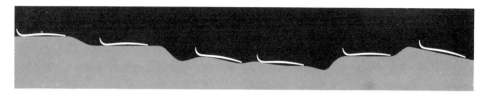

Good: maximum contact between skis and snow.

Poor: insufficient contact; the skis slip on Push-Off.

■ Large moguls

The troughs of large moguls are skied *through*. A Double-Pole Push initiates the descent. The skis are pushed forcefully into the trough and a slight backward lean is assumed. The body swings through with the skis: the arms wind up behind and forcefully swing through low and to the front. At the end of the swing-through action, the arms and poles are well forward and in position for the next pole plant.

■ Small moguls

Depending on the situation (speed, snow condition, wax, etc.), small moguls are either

1 skied over by bringing one ski ahead, thereby lengthening the ski base and reducing snow resistance by spanning the trough,

or

2 strode through whereby a Push-Off is made at the precise instant when the ski spans the mogul. The resulting spring has a catapult effect on the skier.

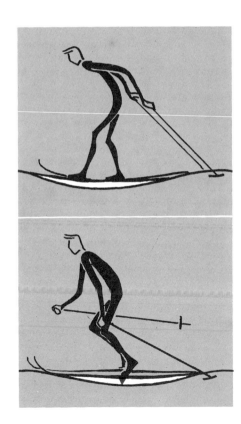

By swinging rhythmically with the skis, the body reinforces adaptation to the terrain. The swinging action of the arms sets the rhythm. In 1, both arms are swung forward simultaneously for the next Double-Pole Push. In 2, the lead arm is swung forward and up extra forcefully.

■ From crests of large moguls or hills
The skier uses a strong Double-Pole Push to initiate the descent. The poles are aimed and planted at the beginning of the decline.

■ Tops of crests or ridges
These are approached quickly and skied over using short, fast strides.

■ Short, steep stretches
These are approached briskly and climbed using short, rapid Diagonal Strides or Jump-Steps.

Chapter 5   Waxes and waxing

The importance of waxes and waxing in the sport of cross-country skiing cannot be overemphasised. The correct choice of wax for specific snow conditions and its proper application are what gives the ski the necessary properties which, when combined with good technique, enable the skier to travel efficiently and with a minimum of effort over the snow. Although the theory and practice of waxing may at first glance appear to be somewhat complex, wax manufacturers have today turned what was once a cultist's "art" into a simple matter of following logical steps and directions. Of course, no theory is absolutely fool-proof, and personal experience is an invaluable asset when it comes to waxing.

■ How wax works

The purpose of wax is to increase the gliding capability of the ski and, at the same time, to enable the ski to grip the snow for the Push-Off and when skiing uphill. These two properties would seem to cancel each other out. However, chemists and wax manufacturers have been able to combine these opposing characteristics into a single wax.

Basically, the principle is a simple one: the base of the ski receives a layer of wax in which the snow crystals become imbedded the instant the weighted ski comes to rest. Sliding the weighted ski over the snow causes friction which generates enough heat to melt the tiny spicules imbedded in the wax and thus releases the ski for the glide.

The wax *sets* prepared under the various commercially available brand names are all based on similar principles. Consequently, aside from minor variations, the information on waxes and waxing contained in this chapter applies to all brands. Always follow the specific instructions which come with each brand. For the all-round and recreational skier, it is recommended that he use the waxes of *one* brand only and get to know their strengths and weaknesses well. The serious competitor, on the other hand, should know that certain waxes of different brands have a decided advantage under specific conditions. Here again, experience is helpful.

■ The snow

The microscopic and gross structure of snow varies and changes due to natural processes. The wax used must adapt as closely as possible to the specific snow condition. Therefore, a thorough examination of the snow characteristics must be made before waxing. First distinguish between *fresh* and *settled* snow:

Fresh snow. Falling or freshly-fallen snow is fluffy. The brittle, hexagonal snow crystals retain their shape for some time. Air trapped between these crystals creates a loosely-packed, fluffy, layer of snow.

Settled snow. After a time, the fresh snow layer settles because the brittle crystals break to form splinters, or melt and then re-freeze to form granules of various sizes. The snow layer drops, becoming more compact, dense and solid.

Different grades of granulation may be distinguished: *fine* — usually found in the upper layers during cold weather; *medium*—found on the surface as powder snow or more often in the bottom half of the snow layer; *large*—found near the ground in old, dry, settled snow and in layers of old, wet snow.

Both fresh and settled snow may be either dry, moist or wet: *dry* snow cannot be readily compressed into a snowball—it falls apart; *moist* snow compresses easily into a firm, solid snowball; *wet* snow drips water when the snow is compressed.

The sharp, brittle spicules of fresh snow crystals dig readily into the wax layer. Therefore, apply a thin layer of wax for fresh snow. Also, the colder the snow, the harder the spicules. Therefore a harder wax is used. Large, hard granules are formed when snow crystals melt and subsequently re-freeze (perhaps repeatedly) into larger configurations. Large granules are found in old, settled snow and have a smoother, more rounded structure

which does not dig well into wax. As a rule, apply a thick layer and use a softer wax on old, settled snow. Extra soft klister (tube or paste wax) is used for crusty, icy and very wet snow.

The cross-country skier must be prepared for a wide variety of snow conditions. Therefore, a *complete* set of waxes and klisters covering the entire range of possible conditions is an integral part of his equipment.

■ **Air temperature**

Waxes are graded according to air temperature and this must be measured before waxing. A thermometer is therefore an absolute necessity for the cross-country competitor and can also be very helpful to the touring skier. Under unstable weather conditions, several readings taken periodically prior to waxing will indicate whether rising, falling or steady temperatures can be expected. The wax is then chosen accordingly.

■ Snow temperature
Snow temperature on the surface corresponds very closely to the air temperature. At ground level, snow temperature usually hovers near the freezing point. However, when rapid changes occur in the air temperature, it may take several hours for the snow surface temperature to follow suit. For example, snow may sometimes still be powdery at temperatures normally indicative of wet snow.

■ The weather
Since air temperature depends on the weather, and snow conditions vary accordingly, it is helpful for the cross-country skier to familiarize himself with the various weather signs. It is not always enough to prepare for existing conditions only as these can alter rapidly and nullify the most painstaking preparation of the skis. Therefore, the over-all weather picture and recent developments should be taken into account.

A complete wax kit

■ The wax kit
A wax kit should include the following items:

— *spatula* (plastic or metal) for scraping off old wax and spreading klisters and the soft dry waxes (in tins) evenly over the base;

— *scraper blade,* usually of stainless steel with sharp edges, to plane smooth, irregular, scratched or damaged ski bases;

— *waxing torch* (special blow torch with an attachment for ironing the wax) used to burn in base tar (Grundvalla), burn off old tar and wax, and warm waxes and klisters;

— *stiff brush* to aid in spreading Grundvalla a n d sometimes warmed klister onto the ski base;

— *Grundvalla (base tar),* which is applied to new or worn skis rendering the base impervious to moisture and improving the adhesion between wax and base;

— *thermometer* to measure air temperature (i.e. snow temperature);

— *complete set of waxes* (preferably of one brand) including base wax, dry waxes (in tins), klisters (in tubes) and some paraffin wax;

— *cork block* to cork (rub smooth) dry waxes;

— *clean, lintless cloth* for wiping off melted wax and excess base tar;

— *cleaning compound* to remove wax from hands, clothing and sometimes ski bases.

■ **Preparing and waxing the skis**

Tarring. Unless already treated, new skis must have their bases tarred before using. Without Grundvalla treatment, moisture enters through the pores of the wood and eventually warps the skis. Grundvalla may be sprayed (aerosol cans) or brushed (bottled form) thinly onto the base. The tar is warmed with the waxing torch and brushed or wiped into the base.

The heat expands the wood pores which are then plugged up with tar. Be careful not to overheat Grundvalla (there should be no smoke or flame). Excess tar is wiped off with a clean cloth. Before applying wax, the base tar must be dry and hard. With heavy use, the base will begin to show blank and exposed areas. It may be necessary to apply Grundvalla two or three times in the course of a season. Before reapplying base tar, be sure to thoroughly clean off old wax and tar.

Also, before storing skis for the summer, clean them thoroughly and apply a new coating of Grundvalla. Occasionally inspect the varnished surfaces of the skis. Sand and re-varnish any chips, scratches or exposed areas as the raw wood will absorb moisture.

Removing Wax. Before waxing, the base must be dry and free from old wax. To remove wax, warm the base with the torch and wipe off the melted wax with a clean rag. To prevent the ski from twisting, gently warm the whole length of the ski first. Special wax-removing compounds are also available.

Waxing. After assessing the snow condition and measuring the air temperature, the appropriate wax is selected.

If possible, wax indoors at room temperature. The waxes will be softer and easier to work with.

Sometimes snow conditions vary greatly along the way, for instance, when passing through alternate shady and sunny areas. Under such conditions, even the most carefully waxed ski will at times be too fast or too slow. However, the skilful skier will compensate by altering his stride accordingly: on fast skis, shorten the stride and push off lightly; on slow skis, keep the ski on the snow and take long strides with powerful Push-Offs.

The ski is supported at the tip with one hand and the wax is applied to the base with the other hand.

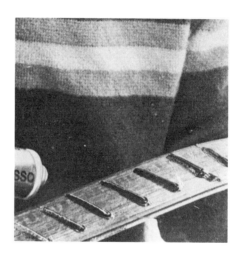

Apply the wax evenly and not in clumps or ridges. Klister is best applied across the ski at regular intervals. The center-groove is kept free of wax and klister. The thickness of the klister layer—dependent on snow conditions—is all-important for a properly waxed ski.

Special touring set of waxes
and klisters

Hard dry waxes are always smoothed by corking. Cork in one direction only, from ski tip to ski heel,

applying light pressure and smooth
strokes. Soft dry waxes and especially klisters (which may be pre-
warmed using the waxing torch)
are smoothed with the heel of the
hand.

Never over-heat waxes or klisters,
producing smoke or bubbles, as
this would destroy their special
properties. Do not use klister while
fresh snow is falling.

A thick layer of wax improves the
climbing capacity of the ski, a thin
layer its gliding quality. Several
thin, well-corked coats applied in
successive layers are generally
more effective than a single, thick
layer of wax.

After waxing, stand the skis upright
in a cold spot (out of doors, in
shade) for at least 10 minutes to
allow the wax to cool and harden.
Then work them in by skiing for 5
to 10 minutes. The full effective-

ness of the wax will then become
apparent.

Waxes may be mixed, provided
they stand next to each other in
the series. For example, Blue with
Green or Blue with Violet is often a
good combination. However, Green
mixed with Violet is not effective. If
the ski feels too fast and does not
grip well on the Push-Off, apply a
thin coat of the next softest wax in
the series to the ski base in the
region below the bindings.

If the ski is too slow and tends to
stick, a harder wax is called for.
Since hard waxes applied over
softer waxes do not usually make
an effective combination, the soft
wax must first be removed.

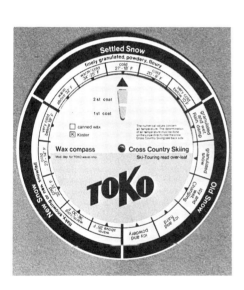

A waxing compass makes waxing
simple

Klisters come in tubes and in
aerosol cans

Dry waxes (in tins) and klisters
(in tubes)

■ Waxing procedures

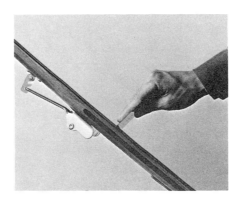

Plane smooth rough or damaged ski bases with scraper blade

Grundvalla (base tar) comes in bottled form or in aerosol cans. The aerosol type with applicator sponge is simple to apply

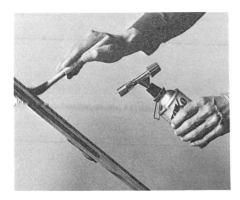

Grundvalla may be warmed with the waxing torch and brushed into the ski base

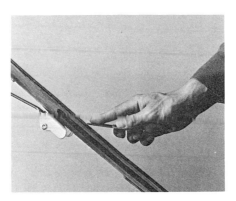

A spatula is used to scrape off old wax and to spread klister (from tubes) evenly over the ski base

Old wax may be warmed with the waxing torch and the fluid wax wiped off with a clean, lintless rag

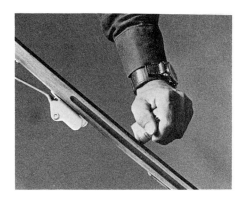

Application of dry waxes (in tins)

Smoothing wax onto base using the waxing torch with the ironing attachment

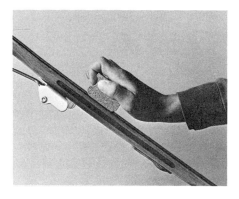

When corking (smoothing) waxes, always stroke from ski tip to ski heel applying light pressure

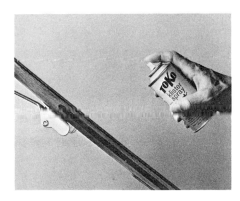

Klisters come in aerosol cans and in tube form.

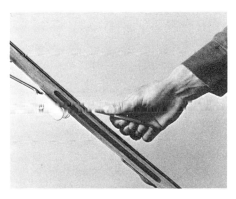

Klister from tubes is spread evenly over the base with a spatula

Smooth klisters with heel of the hand. Stroke from ski tip to ski heel

■ Touring wax chart

TOKO offers a special series of three waxes which are suitable for touring under all conditions (Set Touring). First determine the *dominant* snow characteristics.

Snow structure and temperature	Wax used	Specific use	Application
Falling snow below freezing	TOKO-Minus Blue	For extreme cold, little wax. Thin layer when snowing.	Cork well Cork one layer well, then apply a little more without corking.
Powder snow below freezing	TOKO-Minus Blue	Medium layer for powder or floury snow. The older the snow, the more layers of wax.	Cork each layer well.
Fresh snow and fine granules, moist. Below freezing to +4°C (39° F)	TOKO-Plus Red	Thin layer for moist, thick layer for wet snow.	After application and spreading, TOKO-Plus may be warmed with torch to prevent icing.
Old settled snow— wet, hard or icy, rain, spring snow.	TOKO-Klister Violet + Red-Klister	Apply even layer—thin for fresher snow, thick for large granules. More Red-Klister for wet or icy tracks.	Press klister *evenly* from tube to facilitate spreading an even layer. *Never cork klister.* Tins with applicator sponge may also be used.
Changing snow— hard, wet, powder.	TOKO-Klister Violet TOKO-Minus	Thin layer of klister, TOKO-Minus on top.	If possible, apply klister at room temperature and allow to cool and harden outside or in a cold room. Apply TOKO-Minus using torch *after* klister layer has cooled and hardened.

■ Competition wax chart

This chart should serve as a basis for waxing. Fine points come as a result of experience.

Since the temperature range for the different wax brands are not always exactly identical, average temperature ranges are given here.

Air temperature	Snow structure	Base wax	Running wax	Application
Under —12°C (below 10°F)	Cold fresh or settled powder snow	Green or Special-Green	Green	Thin layers, cork well
—12 to —8°C (10 to 18°F)	Same	Green	Green+Blue	Use a little Blue only when snow is falling
—3 to —8°C (26 to 18°F)	Powder (fresh or settled)	Green	Blue	The lower the temperature, the more Green
0 to —3°C (32 to 26°F)	Fresh snow	Blue	Blue+Violet	Thin layers, *lightly* corked
—1 to +1°C (30 to 34°F)	Fresh, slightly moist snow	Blue, or Blue mixed with Violet	Violet	Thin layers
+1 to +4°C (34 to 39°F)	Fresh, wet snow, and settled, wet snow	Red Yellow	Blue Blue	Thin layer Medium layer
+4°C (39°F) and higher	Fresh, wet, but not falling, snow	Violet-Klister (thin)	Red-Klister	
Below —5°C (21°F)	Crusty or icy snow	Blue-Klister	Blue-Klister + Violet-Klister + thin Red	
Above —5°C (21°F)	Granules	Violet-Klister	Violet-Klister	
Above —2°C (28°F)	Granules	Violet-Klister	Red-Klister	
	Hard track, powder in places	Violet-Klister	Blue (dry)	Cover hardened klister with Blue. Warm with torch.

■ Hints for the use and application of dry waxes and klisters

Special Green (Olive Green): As a rule, apply thinly and cork well; apply paraffin wax to the grooves.

Green and Blue: For settled powder snow, may be smoothed using the ironing attachment with the waxing torch; will result in a better glide, but less grip on uphill stretches.

Blue: Used to advantage on falling snow; use Green as base wax; in heavy snowfall, cork Blue only slightly.

Violet: At temperatures hovering slightly below freezing, apply Violet over a base of Blue; the moister the snow, the more Violet is used. At these temperatures, skis easily become slow or dull. When using Violet, it is wise to test the skis first on open stretches and away from crowds, houses or stadiums which tend to raise the air temperature artificially.

Red: For fresh, wet snow which clumps easily (but not in rain), apply a smooth layer of Red, let harden and then add a layer of Blue on top; warm the wax with the torch to prevent icing.

Yellow: The track often becomes glassy (icy) on fresh, wet snow or on settled snow of fine granules (but not in rain), creating a difficult waxing problem; skis must be perfectly clean of wax remnants as these cause icing; apply a base of Paraffin or hard, Downhill wax, then dab on Yellow and spread evenly with a spatula; finally, apply Blue over the hardened Yellow layer and warm with torch to prevent icing.

Klister: The *thickness* of the klister layer applied is of decisive importance.

Red-Klister: For very wet, soft snow (fresh snow and rain), apply a thin layer using about 1/3 tube; for granules, apply a thicker coat using ½ tube; for wet granules, apply a very thick layer. As a rule, Red-Klister should always be applied over a base of Blue- or Violet-Klister.

Violet-Klister:	An all-round klister for settled snow at temperatures slightly above and below freezing; icy tracks and very moist snow call for thin layer of Red-Klister applied over the Violet to facilitate a powerful Push-Off.
	In the springtime, shaded areas may still be covered in powder snow whereas areas exposed to sunshine have very wet snow. Under these conditions, apply dry Blue wax over a hardened Violet-Klister base and warm with the waxing torch. Do not cork the Blue wax.
Blue-Klister:	Blue-Klister is best suited to icy conditions and hard granules; to facilitate a strong Push-Off, apply some Violet- or Red-Klister over the Blue-Klister.
Base Wax (Nera):	This is used as a base for settled powder snow and to improve adhesiveness of Blue and Green wax; do *not* use on fresh snow as it diminishes glide. As an exception to the rule, it may be used on finely granulated snow at below-freezing temperatures, and results in an excellent ski which will also climb well on icy stretches. However, under no circumstances should the snow be moist.
Grundvalla (Base Tar):	New skis (but not those with synthetic bases) must have their bases thoroughly impregnated with base tar before using. The base must be perfectly clean and dry before applying Grundvalla. Brush or rub the tar into the base with a clean, lintless cloth and warm carefully with the waxing torch for 10 to 15 minutes. Do not overheat tar or scorch the base. Wipe off any excess tar. Repeat Grundvalla treatment when necessary throughout the season and before storing the skis for the summer.

Chapter 6 Training for cross-country skiers

Preparatory training

Although this chapter is mainly intended for the cross-country competitor, the recreational skier will also benefit by following those suggestions which suit him best and for which he can find the time. Physical fitness is a necessary element of good cross country technique and heightens the pure enjoyment of skiing.

Not everyone requires the same amount of training. Physically active individuals will follow a different training and conditioning programme from those who are engaged in sedentary occupations. Success in competition demands a high degree of all-round physical fitness which is built up gradually over several years of intensive conditioning training. Parallel to this foundation training, the ambitious competitor will follow a well-planned, progressive ski-training programme.

The training programmes outlined in this chapter are for the most part too intensive for girls and women. Their work load should be reduced accordingly. The same applies for youngsters. The major portion of their training should consist of long distances interspersed with light speed play (Fartlek Training) as well as specific exercises concentrating on the development of speed. Of great importance is the acquisition of proper technique in the early training stages. Juniors usually learn more readily than older skiers. Young skiers should not "burn themselves out" by competing in too many races in one season.

■ The training rhythm
A skier in training should bear in mind that all living things are subject to *natural rhythms.* Just as late summer and autumn form the peak, and winter the rest period, of the yearly cycle, so the human organism has peak and rest periods throughout the span of his 24-hour day. Obviously, these rhythms must be taken into account if the training is to be effective. The long-term training programme as well as each training session should have warm-up, build-up, peak, cool-off, and rest periods.

A diagrammatic representation of the training rhythm would look like this:

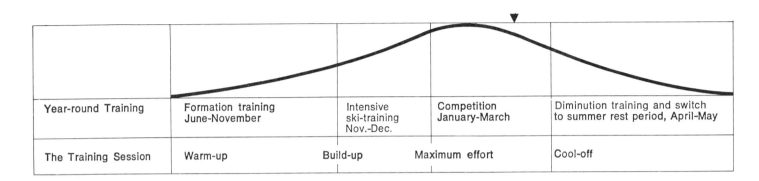

Year-round Training	Formation training June-November	Intensive ski-training Nov.-Dec.	Competition January-March	Diminution training and switch to summer rest period, April-May
The Training Session	Warm-up	Build-up	Maximum effort	Cool-off

Training is aimed at improving the following components of physical fitness:

Agility   Strength   Specific Endurance and Coordination

General Endurance and Coordination   Stamina   Speed

Agility	*Stretch and loosening-up exercises (calisthenics)*	Exercise the entire body concentrating especially on — arms and shoulders — spine, torso and hips — legs
	Special gymnastics	Exercises which improve agility. Use light weights (dumbells, etc.) to increase the load.
Strength	*Weight training for muscle strength*	Heavy weights (⅓ to ½ of own body weight). Concentrate on improving leg strength (knee-bends or squats, standing or lying on back, and vertical jumping from squat position).

Specific Endurance and Coordination	*Special exercises for muscle endurance and coordination*		Use light weights (dumbells and sand bags). Imitation skiing exercises (e.g. slow-motion stride with sand bag behind neck; pulling exercises for the arms using weighted pulleys or rubber slings—1 min. work, 1 min. rest, repeated 6 to 10 times).
General Endurance and Coordination	*Running exercises*	Speed-play (Fartlek)	Longer distances of 3 to 10 km. (2 to 6 mi.) alternating walking, jogging, middle-distance tempo, progressive tempo increase and wind-sprints.
		Interval training	Repeats over distances of 400 to 1500 m. (yds.) (e.g. 10 times 400 m., or 2 sets of 5 times 400 m.) Jog lightly between repeats and increase rest period between sets.
Stamina	*Running exercises*	Cross-country running	Long distances covered in ¾ hr. to 3 hrs. Alternate running and walking. Also use the "ski-stride" especially in advanced training.
		Tempo-training	3,000 to 5,000 m. (2-3 mi.) covered at a steady pace.
Speed	*Running exercises*	Progressive tempo increase	From a light jog, increase tempo gradually to maximum speed and maintain top speed for 20 to 50 m. (yds.) depending on level of condition.
		Wind-sprints	Quick starts and increase to top speed. Distance depending on condition, but not exceeding 80 m. (yds.)
		Repetition training	Repeated sprints of maximum 100 m. (yds.). Rest period between repeats should allow almost complete recovery.

Following are more detailed explanations regarding the various training techniques.

■ Interval training

Rather than covering one long distance at a slow pace, the principle of interval training is to cover many short distances at a fast, controlled pace. The distance, interval of rest, number of repetitions, and time taken to cover the distance can all be varied in order to achieve an optimal training effect. This technique is used to improve specific muscular endurance, coordination, and cardio-respiratory (heart-lung) endurance. During peak efforts, the heart rate should climb to 180 beats per minute in the conditioned athlete. Jog lightly during the rest interval until the heart rate drops to 120/min. and repeat.

■ The ski-stride

This running style imitates the striding action on skis. It is best practiced on gentle uphill stretches. Long, alternating strides are taken concentrating particularly on a powerful push-off from the foot and toes. Occasionally, ski poles are used to simulate the skiing action more closely.

The illustrations demonstrate what the ski-stride should look like. The bottom picture shows how the ground is "gripped": as on skis, the heel should set down first. Also note that a marked hip extension is necessary to attain a long stride. The same applies when skiing.

■ Strength training

Strength training is of utmost importance during the preparatory phase and should also be continued (but reduced) throughout the season between competitions. Weight training equipment should include barbells, dumbells and sandbags. Remember: Improper execution of weight exercises or the use of overly heavy weights can result in injury, especially to the spine. Lift weights with a straight back and use mainly the legs (see diagrams). Leg exercises executed while lying on the back are less dangerous but require a special rack or bench. The cross-country skier should train mainly with light to medium weights and do the exercises rapidly.

The sandbag is placed behind the neck, over the shoulders. Kneebends and alternating deep scissorjumps are excellent exercises for strengthening legs and ankles.

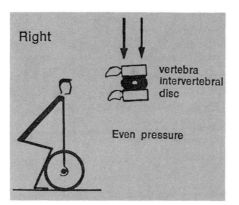

Right

vertebra
intervertebral
disc

Even pressure

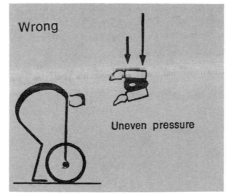

Wrong

Uneven pressure

Barbells may be fashioned from simple materials.

■ Some weekly training programmes

A well-planned foundation training programme should cover about 6 months. If the season commences in December, preparatory training should begin in June. Following are some examples of weekly programmes for this period.

July. 1 to 2 hours, cross-country walking and running, twice a week, plus one session of 2 to 4 hours on Saturdays or Sundays; strong, steady pace interspersed with short middle-tempo stretches; a few minutes of calisthenics out in the open, concentrating on arms and legs; strength training twice a week.

October. 5 days of training per week; cross-country running with speed-play (Fartlek) alternately walking, marching, jogging, running, and sprinting, including 7 to 10 sprints at peak effort; distance may vary, but should always be longer than preferred race distance; use the ski-stride on gentle uphill stretches; concentrate on flexible, powerful spring from the ankles and toes;

One tempo-training session of 3,000 to 5,000 m. (2-3 mi.) at less than maximum pace; daily calisthenics and gymnastic exercises; on strenuous long-distance days, concentrate on flexibility, stretch and loosening exercises, rather than on strength exercises; strength training 2 to 3 times per week.

November (no snow). Similar to October; peak efforts on uphill stretches using ski-stride with poles; 2 tempo sessions over shorter distances of 2,000 m. (1¼ mi.) at higher pace and 200 m. (220 yd.) sprint at the finish; choose a gentle slope 200 to 300 m. (220-330 yds.) long for the ski-stride exercise; after a peak effort, immediately jog back down and continue jogging until sufficiently recovered, then repeat.

■ Points to remember

— Always warm up thoroughly, especially the muscles and joints, before increasing the effort and load. Gradually decrease intensity of effort towards the close of the session (Rhythm!).

— Increase the number of training days gradually. Increase distances in late Summer and early Fall. Aim at building up endurance.

— Increase the intensity of training during Fall. Work harder and faster, but for shorter periods. Increase the number of maximum efforts and gradually decrease the time of the rest interval. Concentrate on speed and quickness in calisthenic and strength training exercises.

— Use the ski-stride more often on hilly terrain, frequently with poles.

— Gradually increase weight in strength-training exercises. Concentrate on push-off and extension power of back, legs and arms.

Gymnastic exercises are best done after the body is warmed up. Time special gymnastics late in the sessions, after the running exercises.

— Whenever possible, train outside and in the open. The cross-country skier must develop a "feel" for the out-of-doors. By

running cross-country on foot, the athlete familiarizes himself with, and adapts to, different weather conditions and variations in the terrain which play a significant role in cross-country skiing.

Old bicycle inner tubes or pulleys with weights may be used to simulate pole work.

Extend arms completely and forcefully.

Training on skis

As snow conditions permit, preparatory dry-land training should gradualy be replaced by training on skis. First concentrate on regaining a feel for the skis, at the same time retaining the condition which has been built up over the preceding months. Dry-land training is modified but continued along with the ski-training.

For the first sessions, lay out a good track, preferably on flat terrain. Find your balance (always weight one ski,) and make *long* strides (good hip extension and long glide). Exaggerate the powerful leg push-off and the final push from the toes. Occasionally skiing without poles will help improve balance and the timing of the arm and leg action.

Once the technique has become well established and automatic again, harder training sessions with increased tempo training, sprints, and shorter uphill efforts may be scheduled. Cross-country running is gradually replaced by tempo- and interval-training on skis. It is of utmost importance to maintain good technique and a relaxed, fluid style, even on peak efforts. Slow down immediately if the movements become forced or cramped. Continue skiing slowly until calm, then gradually pick up pace again.

For speed, coordination, and specific endurance work, a relatively flat, circular track is ideal. For advanced training, work on a gentle uphill stretch about 300 m. (330 yds.) long.

Following is an example of a week's ski-training programme.

December. One long-distance session per week. Include skiing in deep, untracked snow.

Twice a week, repeat uphill runs at peak effort on a fairly steep, but not too long slope. Turn at top, ski down to start and repeat 6 to 10 times.

Tempo-training 1 to 2 times per week. 6-8 repetitions over 600-800 m. (660-880 yds.). Between repeats, ski slowly to recover.

In the latter half of December, include one weekly session of 10 kms. (6¼ mi.) tempo-training at race pace. A challenging and interesting exercise often used in Sweden is to step out of the skis and storm a level or uphill stretch through deep snow on foot.

■ Practical tips

- The best training effect is obtained by competing in races. A skier who has carefully built up to a high level of fitness and condition can compete in many early-season races as a means of preparing for more important events.
- Between competitions, sessions should consist of light ski-training concentrating on a loose, relaxed and fluid style without forcing tempo. Continue stretch and flexibility exercises.
- Continue strength-training 2-3 days after a competition. Training with skiers of similar ability, interests and goals makes hard training more interesting, competitive and enjoyable.
- Train under all weather conditions and even at times when you do not feel quite up to par. Once into the session, weather and queasiness are quickly forgotten.
- It is very important to wax the skis *properly* and *carefully* for each training session. Poorly waxed skis impede proper technique and can even spoil good style.
- Athletes engaged in hard training programmes require sufficient rest. The harder the training, the more you should sleep.

■ Tobacco, alcohol and drugs

It is common knowledge that the use of these compounds is deleterious and can be dangerous to your health. The scientific evidence for this has been well documented and need not be dealt with here. It follows that the time, effort and sacrifice expended in carrying through a long, arduous training programme are too valuable to be wasted by senselessly indulging.

Chapter 7 Competition

The day before the race

If possible, the competitor should arrive early enough to allow for a thorough investigation of the race course. Is it a fast course, or are there many uphill stretches? Does the terrain indicate that a good gliding ski might be of advantage, or do the uphill stretches require a good climbing, but therefore slower, ski? Can downhill stretches be skied at high speed? Is there a turn where time can be saved by cutting the corner? Assess downhill stretches carefully. High speed is desirable to carry the skier as far as possible into the next stretch; however, a fall would waste too much time and should not be risked under any circumstances. Snow and track structure also give indications as to which wax to use. Is the track deep, or is it shallow and ill-defined? Is the snow packed solid, or is it fluffy? Are there icy spots. Does the course lead through alternate sunny and shady areas? Take the time to assess everything carefully. It will pay off during the race.

The evening meal should be taken early. Avoid oily, fried foods. Fat-free, high-protein meat is desirable. High-energy foods should be taken before longer races (30 and 50 kms.). However, do not overload the stomach with such food: a properly trained and conditioned athlete should be able to cover long distances without extra-special food on the eve of his race. After supper, the skis should be prepared. Clean them thoroughly and apply the base wax. If weather conditions are unstable, however, leave the waxing decisions until shortly before the race. Should a hard, frozen, wax-consuming track make a good layer of base wax (i.e. Violet-Klister) seem advantageous, apply this base even though there may be a 90% chance of fresh snow overnight. If the snow has indeed fallen by morning, simply burn off the base. Without fresh snow, however, the highly resistant base will be a decided advantage. For cold, dry, settled snow, prepare the base with Grundvalla and apply Blue or Green after the base tar has cooled and hardened.

While reconnoitering the race course, keep a close watch on temperature and weather. Wind direction and any changes in the upper atmosphere should be noted. The thermometer is hung out before waxing the skis for the observation lap. Take several readings and one before going to bed. If possible, telephone the nearest meteorological information centre and obtain the most recent weather forecast. These steps will help in making the correct decisions for waxing.

Before turning in, take a leisurely evening stroll even though it may be past your accustomed bed-time. Athletes vary in their ability to get a good night's sleep before a race. There are the naturals, who sleep like logs on the evening before their biggest event, and then there are the unfortunate souls who twist and turn restlessly the whole night through, go through the race a thousand times in their tired minds before the break of dawn, and finally sink into a leaden slumber just as the alarm clock jangles. There is no set formula on how to get to sleep on such tension-filled occasions. It is perhaps helpful to turn in somewhat later than usual knowing that a sleepless night is not necessarily the greatest misfortune: a body at rest is able to recover strength and accumulate its reserve energy even without sleep, and the added nervous tension often has a positive effect on performance.

Race-day

Rise early, dress warmly, and go for a brisk walk. This helps wake up mind and body and provides time for a weather check. Have breakfast at least two, preferably three, hours before your event. This allows plenty of time for digestion and waxing the skis. Take a temperature reading and note whether there has been a rise or fall since the last reading. Despite tension and excitement before a race, be sure to wax with utmost care and consideration.

After a visit to the washroom, make any necessary adjustments to your racing uniform and equipment. Tie the start number securely to prevent it from coming undone or hindering your movements. A warm-up suit is worn over the race suit. Begin the warm-up and ski several

kilometers (miles) at a pace which will raise the body temperature sufficiently to ensure optimal function (i.e. work up a good sweat). By this time the wax will begin to show its strengths or weaknesses, and any final corrections are made. When your number is called, you are warmed up, ready to go, and determined to give your competition a good race.

Many suggestions have been made as to the advantages of good tactics during a race. However, no race is ever won on the basis of strategy alone. Superior conditioning and faster skiing will beat any strategy. One suggestion though: collect your energy *before* calling "Track!", and then sprint past your rival strongly and quickly. This will destroy any desire he may have of keeping up to your pace.

The first few kilometers are the most difficult and often decide a race. A maximum effort must be made to overcome your low point and get your second wind. Bear in mind that at this point your opponents also have arms and legs of lead and are gasping for air. If the wax does not quite meet your expectations, especially at temperatures around the freezing mark, don't despair. Adjust your style accordingly and remember that others are experiencing similar difficulties. Under such conditions, the *will to endure* is the deciding factor, and most skiers will cease to be a threat at this point. On downhill stretches, exhale forcefully, emptying the lungs of used air. The last kilometers demand an all-out effort and the last reserve of energy in the finishing sprint. Every second counts.

After crossing the finish, continue skiing slowly and cool down gradually. Then return to retrieve your warm-up suit and head for the showers. Do not loiter about in the cold as the body is very prone to infection in its weakened state. The time for any victory celebrations will come later.

DATE DUE